ideals® EASTER

The daffodils burst forth in spring
in golden shining glory.
And to my mind and heart again
comes Christ's beloved story.
—JOYCE E. DRIVER

IDEALS PUBLICATIONS

NASHVILLE, TENNESSEE

The Coming of Spring

Grace V. Watkins

After the weeks of winter chill,
the warm, sweet gold of a daffodil;
after the silence, white and long,
a little brook's allegro song;
a bird cadenza spilling joy
into the heart of a listening boy;
and shining grass on the wakened sod,
like a lovely psalm of praise to God,
to God who has given you and me
the wonderful gift of eternity.

Spring Offering

Wendy Wagner Tousignant

Today, beneath my windowsill,
Spring offered her first daffodil,
whose flower-head bobbed in the breeze,
then faced the heavens with such ease.

Emerging from dark soil of peat,
her resurrection now complete,
again her head bobbed as if to say,
"Arise with me this Easter Day!"

Photograph © Colette3/Shutterstock

At Easter

Helen E. Maynard

In the time of Resurrection,
all things turn to God.
The tiny seed deep in the earth
bursts upward from the sod.

The trees whose vacant arms
    so long
stood mute against the sky
now flaunt their new dress
    valiantly
and sing, "We did not die."

The emerald grass, the bright
    spring flowers,
the happy birds on wing,
all tell the Easter story
of our risen Lord and King.

Then, heart of mine, you too awake;
cast out all doubt and fear;
roll back the stone—
    hope lives again!—
for Eastertime is here!

Reawakening

Ruth Hazlett

After winter's icy reign,
spring is bursting out again.
Lilt of songbirds fills the air,
new life stirring everywhere.

Robins hopping on the lawn
search for worms at break of dawn;
tulip, crocus, daffodil
bring once more that springtime thrill.

What could more appropriate be—
as these wonders now we see—
than to have glad Easter Day
when the stone was rolled away,

for our hearts to reawaken,
long by slumber overtaken?
Open wide your heart to Him.
Let the Lord of life come in.

Featured Poet

Easter: Hope

Eileen Spinelli

At Easter it is hope
    that greens the grass;
hope that scents
    the tender, tousled air;
hope that takes the weathered silence
    of our hearts
and plants bright music there.

Sun spoons spring
    down wintry roads once more.
We dance in leafy-light,
    by light are led.
Mistakes forgiven—
    we are blessed anew,
our littered griefs behind us—
    grace ahead.

When Spring Is Calling

C. Marecy Boring

What is that mysterious uplift when spring is calling? Is the world about to give over to God? We sense His presence in the violet faces pushing through the brown earth that sheltered them through the long, cold winter. We hear Him in the music of the wild bird's song and feel His touch in the soft, early light that rests on the pussy willow. The world feels a quickening presence, a surge of new life, nearness to the Source of life.

Most of us, perhaps, do not analyze our feelings when spring is calling, but who does not feel a strange pull away from self, from the hustle and bustle we have allowed to hamper our daily living and cloud our vision?

Springtime is a giving over to peace and joy, a feeling of closeness to something divine. Awe and mystery and longing fill the heart. There is a breaking away from routine, a giving over to something beyond everyday physical living, an abandon of our earthly values while we lose ourselves to that intangible something that seems to be all about us.

Spring is calling! The spirit is filled with ecstasy, with sheer joy of being alive, feeling a part of something high and holy and everlasting.

Photograph © Friedrich Strauss/GAP Photos

Expectant Spring

Florence Weberling Rear

Young Spring is dressed in
    shades of green—
so many tints of it are seen,
with a bit of purple here and there
and dots of yellow everywhere.

Her belt is of the brightest blue,
reflection of the sky's clear blue;
her brooch is one red tulip, out
before its time, there is no doubt.

Young Spring is ready now to share
the joy of all who will prepare
to meet with Christ, with thanks to say
to the risen Lord on Easter Day.

Hello, It's Spring

Susan Sundwall

The soldier moss stood up to say,
"I saw a robin yesterday.
And just in case you didn't know,
she said there would be no more snow."

The crocus, being rather shy,
turned her face up to the sky;
with petals opening one by one,
beneath God's shining yellow sun.

The sparrow tossed a song my way;
his warbling simply made my day.
The warming earth, a lovely thing,
God whispering, "Hello, it's spring."

Spring
Celia Thaxter

The alder by the river
shakes out her powdery curls;
the willow buds in silver
for little boys and girls.

The little birds fly over,
and oh, how sweet they sing
to tell the happy children
that once again 'tis spring!

The bright green grass
    comes creeping
so soft beneath their feet;
the frogs begin to ripple
a music clear and sweet.

And buttercups are coming,
and scarlet columbine,
and in the sunny meadows,
the dandelions shine.

And just as many daisies
as their soft hands can hold,
the little ones may gather,
all fair in white and gold.

Here blows the warm red clover;
there peeps the violet blue;
oh, happy little children,
God made them all for you!

My Easter Pay
Mamie Ozburn Odum

Soft Easter winds are singing
around the gabled eaves;
soft clouds resemble snowbanks
against the newborn leaves.
My eyes seek all the glory,
and I hear the echoed thrush—
his rhythm fills the woodland,
with wildflowers growing lush.

And I see a little maiden,
so beautiful, so sweet and fair,

gathering fresh golden daisies,
just the color of her hair.
Skipping near with outstretched hands,
she seeks my rocking chair.
"Oh, Grammy, see how beautiful?
Here's a gift for you to share."

And tiny fingers twining
the fragrant marigold
into my snow-white crown of hair
is ample pay for growing old.

Bits & Pieces

On hillside and in valley,
the warm and gentle rain
awakens sleeping blossoms
to prove Christ lives again.
—*Mabel Marie Wilton*

Easter songs of joyfulness
burst forth with one accord
from hearts abrim with gratitude
to our risen Lord.
—*Mary Boyd Wagner*

Resurrection is a symbol of a perfect life anew,
and each flower that blooms in beauty
breathes God's promises so true.
—*Mary A. Barnard*

*G*od's gift of nature's beauty is a token of His love.
We reciprocate with worship and direct our thoughts above.

—*Ruth Rouse*

*T*he robin sings; the crocuses rise;
God sweeps the land with quiet eyes.
"The Son has risen!" Spring shouts on high.
New life and song now fill the sky.

—*Susan Sundwall*

*W*hen birds are singing in the trees
and flowers blooming on the slope
of woodland hills, then each spring breeze
becomes a messenger of hope.

—*George L. Ehrman*

*Y*e sleeping buds, break
open your green cerements, and wake
to fragrant blossoming for His sweet sake.

—*Margaret French Patton*

Memories of Easter Sundays Gone By

Carol R. Craley

In the northeastern United States, we are still waiting for the first leaves on the trees and for the trees and bushes to flower. Planting season is weeks away and the visual and aromatic signs of spring are not yet evident. This is the time of year this Philadelphia-girl-turned-Mainer relearns the lessons of patience as I sit and wait for nature to come alive again. One location in which spring is in full bloom is the floral department at the grocery store.

As I entered the store yesterday to pick up the last few items for Easter dinner, I was immediately consumed by the smell of lilies—a smell I always associate with Easter. Years of memories came flooding back as I stood next to the heads of lettuce and clementines. I looked next to the lilies at the tulips and other spring flowers. My eyes caught on a display I don't remember seeing for years—small square boxes containing an orchid corsage, always a part of the Easters of my childhood.

Easter was a benchmark. It was an annual "graduation" of sorts, leading to first perfumes, first lipsticks, first kitten heels. Easter Sunday called for a completely new outfit for church—a new suit or dress, with a coordinating hat, of course. If Easter fell too early in the year, a coat was required to go with the dress. Just before the big day, a package would arrive from my great-aunt Margaret containing everything that went *under* the dress. I got my first pair of stockings one Easter Sunday, which meant Great-Aunt Margaret's package included a garter belt too.

Shoes were always an issue, since Mom was a stickler for fashion rules. I knew these would be my only dress shoes for quite a while, so I chose carefully. Some years I wanted white patent leather, rather than the usual black—but wearing white before Memorial Day was a no-no. The purse would match the shoes, and the hat was always a struggle. I've never liked hats—they squashed and messed up my hair, forcing me to leave the hat on all day or take it off and risk my head looking like squirrels had been nesting there. Yet a lady always wore a hat to church. The only year I looked forward to wearing my hat was the year I had picked a Jackie Kennedy–inspired pillbox number to go with my suit. And I always had my white gloves for Easter Sunday, but somehow, soon after Easter, I would manage to lose one—only one—somewhere, and I couldn't wear gloves until next Easter.

Before that glove was lost and my new shiny shoes were scuffed, though, Easter Sunday was a day for photographs. Our family pictures were always taken on the front step of the house. We have home videos, going back to the era of Super 8 film, of the front door opening and family members walking out of the door, pausing, then walking to the cars and waving as they pulled out of the driveway. The other standard spot was by the lamppost in the front yard, the only spot where daffodils were planted. I guess that means I spent my Easter Sundays as a child all decked out, tiptoeing through the daffodils.

Mom's Easter Kindness

Traci Hutcherson

When I was in elementary school, Mom was our Sunday School teacher at church. She loved inviting other little children to come with us.

For a while, every Sunday morning, we would pick up a little girl across town and take her to church with us. She was about five or six years old. I don't remember much about our relationship with this family; I just remember that this little girl's family didn't have much.

Easter Sunday was approaching and this little girl had told Mom that she didn't have a dress to wear on Sunday morning. (She usually wore jeans and a shirt.) Mom asked her what kind of dress she would wear if she had one. The little girl said she had always wanted a pink dress with lots and lots of ruffles. I could see the wheels turning in Mom's head. An amazing seamstress, Mom could sew anything. And her mind was set on making this little girl an Easter dress.

Because Mom was always busy and tended to do things at the last minute (just like me), she started making the dress the night before Easter. I remember going to bed and hearing the whirl of the sewing machine as Mom worked quickly to get the dress sewn before morning.

When I woke up the next morning, I could still hear Mom working on the sewing machine. She was putting the finishing touches on the dress. She had stayed up all night to finish the dress.

Finally it was finished, and Mom held it up for me to see. It was the most beautiful dress! It was pale pink with three or four layers of ruffles in the front. I remember touches of white lace on the sleeves and bottom, and it tied with a big pink bow in the back.

Mom quickly got dressed, and we were off to deliver this Easter surprise to the little girl. She was so excited! She ran in the house to put on her new Easter dress. I don't know who was smiling more—she or Mom (or I!).

That memory found a permanent home in my heart. I saw what joy it brings to do kind things for others. Mom had sacrificed her sleep and her time to bless this little girl, and I saw firsthand the rewards our sacrifices can bring.

Mom had always told me to put the interests of others above my own, but her actions really showed me how to do this. Our actions speak so much louder than our words.

It is an Easter memory I will never forget, and I bet that little girl never will either.

Easter Girl

Lois Donovan

Dear little girl in the Easter bonnet
with a row of posies on it,
tiny gloves and shining feet,
dress of white and smile so sweet:

you are a fragrant flower of spring,
a child who makes my glad heart sing.

I put on a costume I'd made, and I danced at the Easter parade.
We had lots of fun, and that's how I won
good memories that never will fade.
—WILLIAM CLARK

The Easter Bonnet

Mabel F. Hill

Her bonnet was fashioned of flowers and lace,
and its brim was turned up from a round, chubby face.
A blue ribbon bow was tied under her chin,
but that didn't hide a wide, merry grin.
Now, who do you think wore this nice Easter hat?
Why, a wee little maid who was chubby and fat.
Her eyes were as blue as the bow in her hair;
her curls were like cornsilk, so soft and so fair.
The dear little girl with her bonnet of lace
had a look of pure innocence there in her face.

Photograph © J. Cameron Gull/Shutterstock

Our Treasured Traditions

Easter at Grandmother's House

Christa Avampato

When I was little, Easter was my favorite holiday. When I think of the happiest days of my childhood, they all revolve around the Easter dinner table at my grandmother's house. I wish I had told my grandmother how much those days meant to me then, and I wish I had the chance to tell her that they mean even more to me now.

Easter was a special time in that home. The Sharon Rose bush outside would be in full bloom in the front yard. As we pulled into the driveway, my grandmother would be at the door waiting for us to arrive. We were the very best part of her life, and she made sure we knew it every second that she was around us.

The kitchen was the first room we entered in her home, and there was always a glorious, welcoming scent coming from the oven. On Easter, it was lamb—a dish I had nowhere else and at no other time of year. It would be accompanied by potatoes, glazed carrots, and buttered peas. Everyone got their own individual salad in their own individual bowl, which I always got a kick out of. And my grandfather and I would put black olives on our fingertips—the olives too big for my fingers and too small for his—and then we would wave at each other.

Once the dishes had been cleared and washed, my favorite part of the meal would start. My grandmother would make her way over to the fridge and use the step stool to grab a large, round Tupperware container. Inside would be her special cake that I always thought she made just for me. It was incredibly simple—a yellow cake made from a mix topped with sliced cinnamon apples. It's still my very favorite food in the world, and I've never been able to re-create it exactly as she made it. There was something special about that cake—I think it was all the love she put into it.

The coffee would start brewing, the walnuts and the nutcracker would come out, and then the stories would start spilling from everyone. Most of them were about people whom I'd never met, relatives who had passed on long before I was born, but through all of those stories I came to know them and love them as much as I loved all

of the people around that table. I'd grab another slice of cake and hope that somehow that dinner could go on forever.

Long after the sun went down, we'd pile back into the car with leftovers in tow and make the long drive back to our house. My grandmother would be at the door, waving goodbye and staring out into the darkness long after our car was out of view.

Though today I'm spending Easter in a much different way than I did all those years ago, my mind is traveling back in time to that table surrounded by those people. I'm so grateful for the time we all had the chance to be together.

Family Recipes

Classic Carrot Cake

- 2 cups all-purpose flour
- 2 teaspoons baking powder
- 2 teaspoons baking soda
- 2 teaspoons ground cinnamon
- ½ teaspoon salt
- 2 cups granulated sugar
- 4 eggs
- ½ cup vegetable oil
- 2 cups grated carrots
- 1 cup drained, crushed pineapple
- ½ cup flaked coconut
- ½ cup chopped walnuts
  Cream-Cheese Frosting, recipe below

Preheat oven to 350°F. In a medium bowl, sift together flour, baking powder, baking soda, cinnamon, and salt. Mix in granulated sugar; set aside. In a large bowl, beat 4 eggs; stir in vegetable oil, carrots, crushed pineapple, coconut, and walnuts. Add dry ingredients; mix well. Spoon into 3 greased and floured 8-inch round cake pans. Bake 30 to 35 minutes. Remove and cool in pans 10 minutes; remove from pans to wire racks and cool completely. Spread frosting between cake layers and on top and sides. Makes 12 to 16 servings.

Cream-Cheese Frosting

- ½ cup butter, softened
- 1 8-ounce package cream cheese, softened
- 1 teaspoon vanilla extract
- 1 pound confectioners' sugar, sifted

In a large bowl, combine butter, cream cheese, and vanilla. Slowly add confectioners' sugar. Mix well. Spread onto cake or cover and refrigerate until ready to use. Makes about 4 cups.

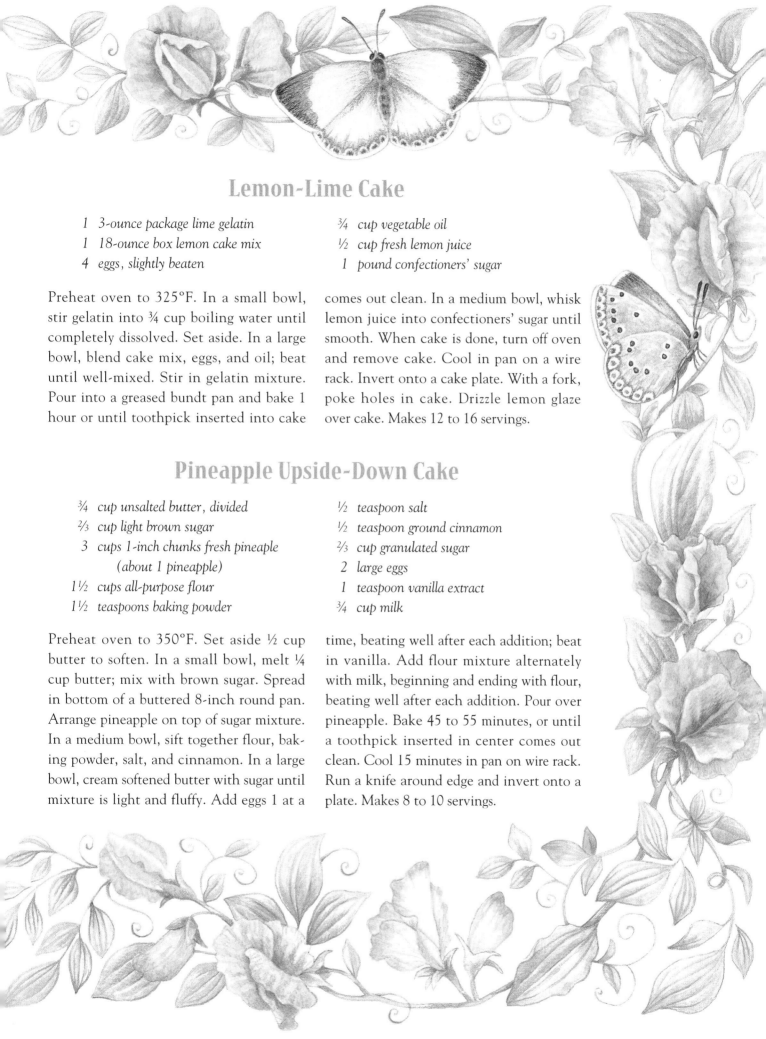

Lemon-Lime Cake

1 3-ounce package lime gelatin
1 18-ounce box lemon cake mix
4 eggs, slightly beaten
¾ cup vegetable oil
½ cup fresh lemon juice
1 pound confectioners' sugar

Preheat oven to 325°F. In a small bowl, stir gelatin into ¾ cup boiling water until completely dissolved. Set aside. In a large bowl, blend cake mix, eggs, and oil; beat until well-mixed. Stir in gelatin mixture. Pour into a greased bundt pan and bake 1 hour or until toothpick inserted into cake comes out clean. In a medium bowl, whisk lemon juice into confectioners' sugar until smooth. When cake is done, turn off oven and remove cake. Cool in pan on a wire rack. Invert onto a cake plate. With a fork, poke holes in cake. Drizzle lemon glaze over cake. Makes 12 to 16 servings.

Pineapple Upside-Down Cake

¾ cup unsalted butter, divided
⅔ cup light brown sugar
3 cups 1-inch chunks fresh pineaple
   (about 1 pineapple)
1½ cups all-purpose flour
1½ teaspoons baking powder
½ teaspoon salt
½ teaspoon ground cinnamon
⅔ cup granulated sugar
2 large eggs
1 teaspoon vanilla extract
¾ cup milk

Preheat oven to 350°F. Set aside ½ cup butter to soften. In a small bowl, melt ¼ cup butter; mix with brown sugar. Spread in bottom of a buttered 8-inch round pan. Arrange pineapple on top of sugar mixture. In a medium bowl, sift together flour, baking powder, salt, and cinnamon. In a large bowl, cream softened butter with sugar until mixture is light and fluffy. Add eggs 1 at a time, beating well after each addition; beat in vanilla. Add flour mixture alternately with milk, beginning and ending with flour, beating well after each addition. Pour over pineapple. Bake 45 to 55 minutes, or until a toothpick inserted in center comes out clean. Cool 15 minutes in pan on wire rack. Run a knife around edge and invert onto a plate. Makes 8 to 10 servings.

Easter Hospitality

Kristi J. West

One Palm Sunday, a number of years ago, a woman from my church approached me and asked if I had any plans for Easter dinner. My plan at that point was simple: warming up leftovers and a quiet afternoon with my feline companion. Living far from family meant sometimes sacrificing treasured family gatherings due to work obligations. Since I had not made any formal plans, and I knew my cat wouldn't mind, I accepted her invitation to have Easter dinner with her family the following Sunday.

I was a little nervous about being the outsider at an Easter family gathering, but I was welcomed graciously. As dinner was prepared, the adults enjoyed the warmth of the sun, lively conversation, and a cool glass of lemonade on the patio while controlled chaos came from the children of the home. We eventually gathered around the large table, and my hostess's husband said a blessing before we ate. Traditional Easter fare of ham, potatoes, and rolls were enjoyed. What I was not expecting with dinner was a question-and-answer session or the family tradition that followed. I've since learned that my hostess always incorporates deep conversation into all family gatherings, much to the chagrin of the children. After an interview about my own family's Easter rituals,

"Resurrection eggs" were brought to the table. These brightly colored plastic eggs contained a miniature symbol of Easter and an explanation of that biblical object inside.

The carton of eggs was passed around the table and each person took a colored egg. Each egg was numbered from one through twelve. We each took a turn—breaking open our egg, sharing the object hidden inside our egg, and reading aloud about our miniature treasures. Three small coins represented the money paid to Judas for his betrayal. Denoting the crown of thorns on Jesus' head was a thorn broken off the stem of a rose. A rock symbolized the stone that was rolled away from Jesus' tomb. The twelfth egg was empty. It represented the empty tomb and Jesus' Resurrection. It was such a touching and visual way to tell the story of Easter. Each person around the table became a storyteller, playing his or her part in the retelling of the Easter story. What an interesting way to end Easter dinner!

That Easter became a treasured holiday memory for me. The kindness extended to me by this family and others is a wonderful example of hospitality and generosity: "I was a stranger, and you invited me into your home" (Matthew 25:35).

Easter Message

Luella Bender Carr

The window in the choir loft caught
and held the morning sun,
became a square of pebbled golden light.
The pictured cross upon it
held one lovely spray
of flawless Easter lilies, waxen white.

As I listened to the sermon
or the choir again, again,
my eyes, despite my will,
would stray and linger on the pane,
that pointed golden panel
with the lilies snowy, pure.
And the painted cross behind them
held a message to assure
me of God's love and mercy.
The sunlit window gleamed.
As I raised my head from praying,
God was smiling—so it seemed.

By an Open Church Window

Gwen Roberts Boyer

Music of the birds I hear,
birds on bush and tree,
blended with the preacher's voice—
both are calling me!
Springtime with her many lures
make my senses wander;
yet the parson's simple words
cause my heart to ponder.
Songs to God this day inspires—
sung by birds and human choirs.

The Holy Season
Virginia Blanck Moore

The holy season's here again—
the lilies burst and bloom,
and faith lights up the troubled hearts
and banishes the gloom.

The holy season's here again—
the tomb is empty, bare;
and jubilation fills the minds
of Christians everywhere.

The holy season's come again—
the stone is rolled away;
and love and hope and faith rise up
to greet the Easter Day!

Lenten Trip
Margaret Rorke

As earth draws closer to the sun
to warm its frozen sod,
all Christian hearts prepare as one
for closeness to their God.
The roads of faith this time of year
retrace where Jesus went
and bring His presence very near
these holy days of Lent.

Oh, blest is he who makes the trip—
whatever be his means—
whose mind and soul he will equip
to see and feel the scenes

our Savior knew so long ago,
undulled by passing time,
inviting all who want to know
the height of the sublime.

The trav'ler views the glens of good,
eternal rocks of love,
the source of Christian brotherhood,
the hope-capped hills above
the streams that flow with lasting peace—
all this is on the way
for those whose journey does not cease
till dawn on Easter Day.

The Triumphal Entry

Clay Harrison

Jesus entered Jerusalem on an unridden donkey,
descending from the Mount of Olives for the multitudes to see.
They rejoiced and loudly praised Him for mighty works He'd done,
but they still were unaware that He was God's own Son!

He had raised Lazarus from the grave; now the Passover was near,
but it was not mere circumstance that was bringing Him here.
The people shouted, "Hosanna! Blessed is the one who comes!"
It was a simple celebration with no fanfare or drums.

The people waved palm branches, spread garments in His path,
before He entered the temple, where they would feel His wrath.
The Pharisees rebuked Him when they heard the people shout.
Jesus said, "If these were silent, the stones would cry out!"

Hosanna in the Highest!

Alice Kennelly Roberts

They spread their garments o'er His path
on that great festive day;
they cut down branches from the trees
and strewed them o'er the way.

And voices cried aloud in song
of adoration, praise,
to say that this was, in their lives,
the happiest of days.

How quickly doth the wind reverse
from balmy breeze to chill!
How suddenly men's hearts are changed;
the crowd is fickle still.

And so, the One whom they adored
with every cheering breath,
was quickly turned and spat upon,
and then—condemned to death!

Betrayal in the Garden

Robert F. Gruenewald

As they waited in the garden,
a multitude appeared,
with swords and staves and torches,
in search of Him they feared.

Forth from the crowd strode Judas,
"Hail, Master," was his cry,
and kissed the Lord he followed,
betrayed Him then to die.

"Friend, wherefore art thou come?"
said Jesus that dread night,
but then they came and took Him,
His disciples taking flight.

They led Him to the high priest,
where some came to deride,
and scribes and elders cursed Him,
then held Him to be tried.

Jesus Went Out to a Garden

Carolyn Winfrey Gillette

Jesus went out to a garden
to a quiet place to pray.
In the night, a crowd came round Him,
led by Judas on their way.
They seized Jesus to arrest Him;
someone near then drew a sword.
Soon a servant was injured,
suffering there beside our suffering Lord.
Jesus spoke to stop the violence:
"Put your sword back in its place."
Then He touched the servant and healed Him
in a moment filled with grace.
For as violence leads to violence
causing more distress and pain—
So compassion in abundance
is a witness to God's reign.

God of love, we pause and wonder:
did that servant give quiet praise?
Yet the story marches onward
with the pain that it portrays.
For the One who brought such healing
soon was broken, on a cross,
to our sinful world revealing
violence has an awful cost.
God, the Gospels bear a witness:
Your Son's death was not the end.
By Your grace, You raised up Jesus;
sin and violence did not win.
May we work to end all suffering;
lead us in Christ's peaceful way.
May His peace become an offering
that we share throughout each day.

THE LAST SUPPER AND THE GARDEN OF GETHSEMANE

Mark 14: 12–26, 32–42

And the first day of unleavened bread, when they killed the passover, his disciples said unto him, Where wilt thou that we go and prepare that thou mayest eat the passover?

And he sendeth forth two of his disciples, and saith unto them, Go ye into the city, and there shall meet you a man bearing a pitcher of water: follow him. And wheresoever he shall go in, say ye to the goodman of the house, The Master saith, Where is the guestchamber, where I shall eat the passover with my disciples? And he will shew you a large upper room furnished and prepared: there make ready for us.

And his disciples went forth, and came into the city, and found as he had said unto them: and they made ready the passover.

And in the evening he cometh with the twelve. And as they sat and did eat, Jesus said, Verily I say unto you, One of you which eateth with me shall betray me.

And they began to be sorrowful, and to say unto him one by one, Is it I? and another said, Is it I?

And he answered and said unto them, It is one of the twelve, that dippeth with me in the dish. The Son of man indeed goeth, as it is written of him: but woe to that man by whom the Son of man is betrayed! good were it for that man if he had never been born.

And as they did eat, Jesus took bread, and blessed, and brake it, and gave to them, and said, Take, eat: this is my body.

And he took the cup, and when he had given thanks, he gave it to them: and they all drank of it. And he said unto them, This is my blood of the new testament, which is shed for many. Verily I say unto you, I will drink no more of the fruit of the vine, until that day that I drink it new in the kingdom of God.

And when they had sung an hymn, they went out into the mount of Olives. . . .

And they came to a place which was named Gethsemane: and he saith to his disciples, Sit ye here, while I shall pray.

And he taketh with him Peter and James and John, and began to be sore amazed, and to be very heavy; And saith unto them, My soul is exceeding sorrowful unto death: tarry ye here, and watch. And he went forward a little, and fell on the ground, and prayed that, if it were possible, the hour might pass from him.

And he said, Abba, Father, all things are possible unto thee; take away this cup from me: nevertheless not what I will, but what thou wilt. And he cometh, and findeth them sleeping, and saith unto Peter, Simon, sleepest thou? couldest not thou watch one hour? Watch ye and pray, lest ye enter into temptation. The spirit truly is ready, but the flesh is weak. And again he went away, and prayed, and spake the same words.

And when he returned, he found them asleep again, (for their eyes were heavy,) neither wist they what to answer him.

And he cometh the third time, and saith unto them, Sleep on now, and take your rest: it is enough, the hour is come; behold, the Son of man is betrayed into the hands of sinners. Rise up, let us go; lo, he that betrayeth me is at hand.

Stained glass window in Iquique, Chile. Photograph © jorisvo/Shutterstock

THE CRUCIFIXION AND BURIAL

John 19:25–42

Now there stood by the cross of Jesus his mother, and his mother's sister, Mary the wife of Cleophas, and Mary Magdalene. When Jesus therefore saw his mother, and the disciple standing by, whom he loved, he saith unto his mother, Woman, behold thy son! Then saith he to the disciple, Behold thy mother! And from that hour that disciple took her unto his own home.

After this, Jesus knowing that all things were now accomplished, that the scripture might be fulfilled, saith, I thirst. Now there was set a vessel full of vinegar: and they filled a spunge with vinegar, and put it upon hyssop, and put it to his mouth.

When Jesus therefore had received the vinegar, he said, It is finished: and he bowed his head, and gave up the ghost.

The Jews therefore, because it was the preparation, that the bodies should not remain upon the cross on the sabbath day, (for that sabbath day was an high day,) besought Pilate that their legs might be broken, and that they might be taken away. Then came the soldiers, and brake the legs of the first, and of the other which was crucified with him. But when they came to Jesus, and saw that he was dead already, they brake not his legs: But one of the soldiers with a spear pierced his side, and forthwith came there out blood and water. And he that saw it bare record, and his record is true: and he knoweth that he saith true, that ye might believe. For these things were done, that the scripture should be fulfilled, A bone of him shall not be broken. And again another scripture saith, They shall look on him whom they pierced.

And after this Joseph of Arimathaea, being a disciple of Jesus, but secretly for fear of the Jews, besought Pilate that he might take away the body of Jesus: and Pilate gave him leave. He came therefore, and took the body of Jesus. And there came also Nicodemus, which at the first came to Jesus by night, and brought a mixture of myrrh and aloes, about an hundred pound weight.

Then took they the body of Jesus, and wound it in linen clothes with the spices, as the manner of the Jews is to bury. Now in the place where he was crucified there was a garden; and in the garden a new sepulchre, wherein was never man yet laid. There laid they Jesus therefore because of the Jews' preparation day; for the sepulchre was nigh at hand.

Stained glass window in San Jeronimo el Real Church in Madrid, Spain. Photograph © Marques/Shutterstock

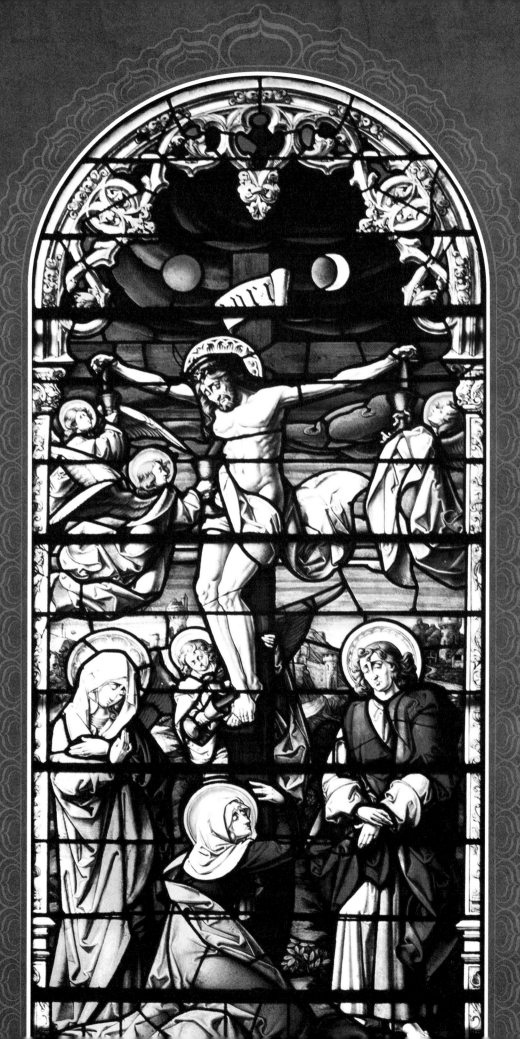

The Empty Tomb and What Mary Saw

John 20:1–18

The first day of the week cometh Mary Magdalene early, when it was yet dark, unto the sepulchre, and seeth the stone taken away from the sepulchre. Then she runneth, and cometh to Simon Peter, and to the other disciple, whom Jesus loved, and saith unto them, They have taken away the Lord out of the sepulchre, and we know not where they have laid him. Peter therefore went forth, and that other disciple, and came to the sepulchre. So they ran both together: and the other disciple did outrun Peter, and came first to the sepulchre. And he stooping down, and looking in, saw the linen clothes lying; yet went he not in. Then cometh Simon Peter following him, and went into the sepulchre, and seeth the linen clothes lie, And the napkin, that was about his head, not lying with the linen clothes, but wrapped together in a place by itself. Then went in also that other disciple, which came first to the sepulchre, and he saw, and believed.

For as yet they knew not the scripture, that he must rise again from the dead. Then the disciples went away again unto their own home.

But Mary stood without at the sepulchre weeping: and as she wept, she stooped down, and looked into the sepulchre, And seeth two angels in white sitting, the one at the head and the other at the feet, where the body of Jesus had lain.

And they say unto her, Woman, why weepest thou? She saith unto them, Because they have taken away my Lord, and I know not where they have laid him. And when she had thus said she turned herself back, and saw Jesus standing, and knew not that it was Jesus.

Jesus saith unto her, Woman, why weepest thou? whom seekest thou? She, supposing him to be the gardener, saith unto him, Sir, if thou have borne him hence, tell me where thou hast laid him, and I will take him away.

Jesus saith unto her, Mary. She turned herself, and saith unto him, Rabboni; which is to say, Master. Jesus saith unto her, Touch me not; for I am not yet ascended to my Father: but go to my brethren, and say unto them, I ascend unto my Father, and your Father; and to my God, and your God.

Mary Magdalene came and told the disciples that she had seen the Lord, and that he had spoken these things unto her.

Jesus Makes Breakfast

(A POEM ABOUT JOHN 21:1–14)

Carol Penner

I could smell that charcoal fire a long way off,
while we were still rowing far from shore.
As we got closer I could smell the fish cooking;
I imagined I could hear it sizzling.
When you're hungry, your mind works that way.

When the man by the fire asked us about our catch,
we held up the empty nets.
And His advice to throw the nets in once more
is something we might have ignored,
except for the smell of cooking fish—
this guy must know something about catching fish!

The catch took our breath away;
never in my life have we pulled so many in one heave.
I was concentrating on the catch,
but John wasn't even paying attention.
He was staring at the shore
as if his life depended on it.
Then he clutched my shoulder, crying,
"It is the Lord!"

Suddenly, everything came into focus—
the man, the catch, the voice;
and nothing could stop me,
I had to be with the Master.

There were no words at breakfast,
beyond, "Pass the fish,"
or "I'll have a bit more bread."
We sat there, eating our fill,
basking in the sunrise.
We didn't have to say anything.
Jesus just smiled and served.

The Story of a Song

Easter Anthem

Pamela Kennedy

Charles Wesley was one of the most prolific hymn writers of all time, contributing more than 6,500 hymn texts to Christian tradition. Born in Lincolnshire, England, he was the youngest of eighteen children. His father, Samuel, was a poor country parson, and his mother, Susannah, lived as a model of Christian piety and organization who spent at least two hours each day in prayer.

After his early education at home, Charles attended Westminster School in London and later Christ Church College, Oxford. While there he met with other young men who, because of their strict rules and methods for living, studying, and practicing Christianity, become known as Methodists. His intellectual and orderly approach to faith, however, would soon be tested in the world outside academia.

In 1735, after his ordination as an Anglican priest, Charles was sent to British North America to serve as secretary to General Oglethorpe, the governor of the colony of Georgia. Charles failed to distinguish himself in this position and within a year was on his way back to England. Caught in a violent storm, his ship began taking on water at an alarming rate. Praying for God's mercy, Wesley recorded the following: "In this dreadful moment, I bless God, I found the comfort of hope; and such joy in finding I could hope, as the world could neither give nor take away." Within eighteen months, safely ashore back in England, Wesley's faith was challenged once again. Near death from dysentery and pleurisy, he wrote in his diary, "I labored, waited, and prayed to feel 'Who loved me, and gave Himself for me.'" Not much later, after experiencing what he considered a divine healing, he journaled, "I now found myself at peace with God and rejoiced in hope of loving Christ." The fires of evangelism thus fanned, Charles became an itinerant preacher and soon attracted a large following.

Within a year or so, Wesley purchased a deserted cannon foundry as a more permanent home for his growing congregation. And on Easter Sunday, 1739, the congregants in London's first Wesleyan chapel sang the hymn Charles composed for their inaugural service: "Hymn for Easter Day." We know it as "Christ the Lord Is Risen Today." Shortly after its composition, in order to accommodate the melody, an anonymous writer added the *alleluias* we now sing at the end of each verse.

Today, more than 250 years after the song's composition, Christians everywhere still greet each new Easter morning with Wesley's joyful declaration: "Christ the Lord is risen today!"

"Christ the Lord Is Risen Today"

by Charles Wesley (1707–1788)

If You Love Me, Feed My Sheep

Honoria A. Groves

Jesus spoke these words to Peter
on the shores of Galilee:
"Feed My flocks—they are so needy—
if you truly care for Me.

"Seek the wandering and wayward—
as I sought and cared for thee—
only if you have compassion,
if you have real love for Me.

"Care for those who need a Shepherd:
lead them to the pastures green;
guide them to such living water
as their eyes have never seen."

Yes, I love You, blessed Shepherd.
You have done so much for me.
Help me spread Your love to others—
Your salvation may they may see.

Red barn and blooming tree near Colfax, Washington.
Photograph © Dennis Frates Photography.
Inset above: photograph © Karel Gallas/Shutterstock

A Broken Chrysalis

Dr. Ralph F. Wilson

It's truly amazing what a girl will do for love. My wife, Jean, and I lived next door to each other for ten years before we were married. My interest in high school biology had sparked a live caterpillar collection. Their home was a shoe box, covered with screen wire. When I went on vacation, Jean fed them faithfully with leaves from her willow tree. She hated it.

Finally the caterpillars stopped their incessant crawling and chewing, attached their tails firmly to a stick and lay still, sheathed with a shiny leather-like case. For weeks they seemed to be dead, unmoving in their tiny gray wrappings. I removed the screen and waited.

One by one, the gray cases began to twist and turn violently and suddenly split open. A beautiful butterfly emerged. It stood for hours gently moving its wings, pumping fluids into them to extend them fully. Then the butterfly soared gracefully away on the breezes of summer, leaving nothing behind but a broken chrysalis to indicate its former bondage.

The chrysalis and butterfly suggest the empty graveclothes of our risen Lord. When Peter and John heard the news that the Lord's body was gone from the garden tomb, they ran all the way from their lodging. Peter entered the tomb and "saw the strips of linen lying there, as well as the burial cloth that had been around Jesus' head. The cloth was folded up by itself, separate from the linen" (John 20:6–7, NIV 1984). The graveclothes once wrapped continuously around the body now lay collapsed, mute testimony that the corpse they had once shrouded had now emerged in life.

The bondage of death is broken. Christ is risen! We can face tomorrow with the assurance that Jesus is in fact alive to help us, to guide us, to give us hope for the future. And since He is living, our problems are not insolvable. The broken chrysalis of His graveclothes proclaims that Christ is victor even over death. Because He lives, nothing is impossible.

Photograph © Radius/SuperStock

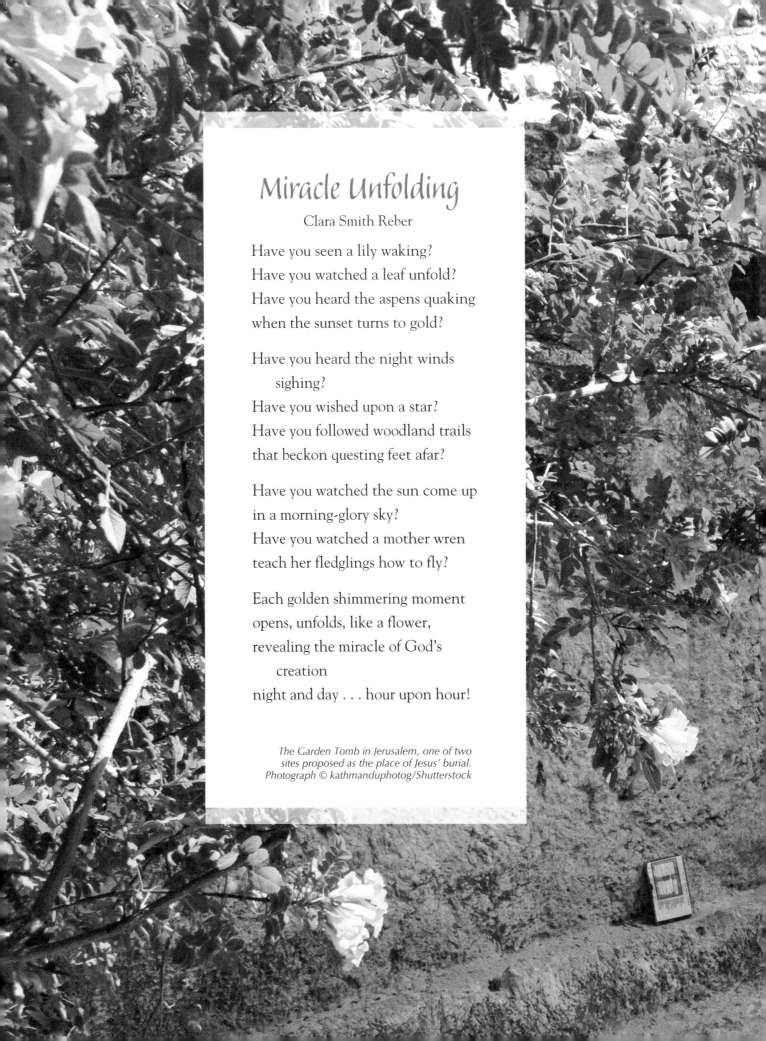

Miracle Unfolding

Clara Smith Reber

Have you seen a lily waking?
Have you watched a leaf unfold?
Have you heard the aspens quaking
when the sunset turns to gold?

Have you heard the night winds
    sighing?
Have you wished upon a star?
Have you followed woodland trails
that beckon questing feet afar?

Have you watched the sun come up
in a morning-glory sky?
Have you watched a mother wren
teach her fledglings how to fly?

Each golden shimmering moment
opens, unfolds, like a flower,
revealing the miracle of God's
    creation
night and day . . . hour upon hour!

*The Garden Tomb in Jerusalem, one of two
sites proposed as the place of Jesus' burial.
Photograph © kathmanduphotog/Shutterstock*

Through My Window

Everyday Easters

Pamela Kennedy

This is an unusual Easter story because it began in July. A few days after the Fourth, we invited some friends over for dinner, and they called to say they couldn't come because they were going through a "nightmare." They were staying at their beach house with all their family (three grown kids, three spouses, two young grandsons, and three dogs). On Friday evening, neighbors brought over some leftover fireworks and just as one particularly loud aerial display went off, someone opened the door and, well here it is from their email: "Xoco (Bryce, Malissa, and Brock's dog) bolted and took off like a rocket into the back woods. We looked for him for a couple of hours. Bryce and Malissa till about 3:00 A.M. The search continued today, and we put out a ton of flyers and roamed by car and foot. The search stopped at 9:30 this evening. Still no sign of him. I don't know what the plan is for tomorrow or Monday, but we're all short on sleep and praying for a miracle."

The lost dog is a xoloitzcuintli (Mexican hairless) and lives in the city. The area surrounding the beach house is wooded and home to raccoons, skunks, foxes, and the occasional bear. Things didn't look good for Xoco. Sunday passed with no sign of the runaway. Some family members had to go back to work, but Malissa and her seven-year-old son, Brock, stuck around, as did her in-laws, our friends, Denny and Jenna. Monday, three days after the "great escape," Jenna took Brock to the nearest town for lunch, leaving Denny and Malissa at the cabin.

Malissa was distraught and discouraged but, unwilling to give up the increasingly hopeless search for her dog, she wandered along the rural two-lane highway. Around noon a car stopped beside her and asked if she had a phone. They were holding one of the "Lost Dog" flyers and said they thought they had just seen the dog a mile or so down the road and wanted to call the owners. "He's mine!" she yelped, and they quickly told her where they had spotted him. Malissa ran back to the cabin, grabbed Denny, and they hopped into the car. At the designated location, Malissa got out and started calling for Xoco, to no avail. Then Denny looked in his rearview mirror and thought he caught a glimpse of something black dashing away from the highway down a dirt road. He called to Malissa, who jumped back into the car; they made a quick U-turn. About fifty yards down the side road, in the underbrush, they spotted something. Malissa dashed out of the car, called and whistled for Xoco, and the scratched and dirty dog barreled through the tangled weeds and leapt into her arms. Her relief and pent-up fear exploded into sobs as she sank to her knees,

cradling her wriggling pet. It was, Denny related to us later, "sort of like a resurrection . . . that same kind of amazed joy."

And that's where Easter comes in. I got to thinking about how many times, all through the year, God reveals Himself to us in resurrection experiences—everyday Easters, if you will. We lose something important—a job, a relationship, our health, our hope. In our despair, we pray for guidance, for restoration, to find our way again. We work to make things right, but when it doesn't happen in the way or in the time frame we expect, it's hard to keep going. Then, sometimes slowly, but sometimes suddenly, that thing that seemed dead returns to life—we are offered a new opportunity we couldn't have imagined. A relationship is mended through forgiveness and grace. We experience healing. Our hope is restored in unexpected ways.

When Jesus said, "I am the resurrection and the life" (John 11:25, NKJV), I don't think He was just talking about physically raising folks from the dead in the future (although He certainly promises that). The declaration is in the present tense. It happens in this life. His resurrection power includes earthly hopes and dreams, as well as earthly bodies. He restores those lost in pain and despair and those lost in sin and shame—here and now. He grants blinded eyes as well as blinded minds new vision, as believers trust in Christ. Some resurrections are small and some are huge, but in each experience our faith is expanded and our hearts fill once again with the amazed joy of Easter. It happens every day.

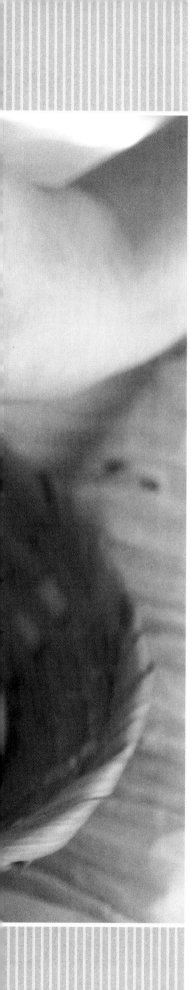

A New Beginning

Ramona K. Cecil

Spring is like a new beginning
when the earth seems
    fresh and clean,
when the air is full of blossoms
and the world is new and green.

It's like God has said, "Start over,
leave old doubts and fears behind.
Anything is possible—
just seek and you will find."

When I smell the fragrant lilacs
and I hear the robins sing,
I think God puts a little Eden
in the making of each spring.

You feel there's naught
    you can't accomplish—
there's nothing you can't do—
when the air is full of blossoms
and the world is green and new.

Easter Is a Promise Fulfilled

Johnielu Barber Bradford

Each Easter is a promise of life fulfilled
and all of nature takes a part;
the resurrection of springtime's rebirth
overwhelms the joyful heart.

Easter comes with cadence of new hope;
the songs of cardinals in the trees
and fragrant blooms of apple, plum, and peach
call forth the buzzing honeybees.

Oh, the wonder of God's handiwork—
His touch revives the crocus beds;
He gently wakes the sleeping Easter lilies
and crowns the yellow iris heads!

Easter is a promise of new beginnings;
wild violets with perfumed breath
emerge from winter's bier victoriously—
life, triumphant over death.

Living Again and Again

George Matthew Adams

Springtime shall always remain for me the most inspiring season of the year. Each new one is an added endorsement of the feasibility of an abundant faith and an ever-present Creator and Guardian over all.

Each morning I take the same interest and happy speculation as to each day's new growth of bud and flower. I saw the leaves of autumn color and fall gently to the ground and hover closer to the earthly Mother of us all. I saw the green grass curl and creep into the soil for a winter rest. I saw the stripped trees, naked and lonely, bending under the wind and storm of many a melancholy day.

But as the beauty and fragrant foliage of departed springs leave a memory behind, so is anticipation stirred anew over each one's return. Even the same season is never quite the same, any more than our dearest friend is the same every time we meet him. But the soul of each is changeless.

We should be encouraged by each spring's return. It helps to fortify our own faith in the permanence of the life of the soul, and adds to our joy over what we may have planted of ideas or acts in the lives of others.

It is the privilege of us all to live on—again and again—in newer and better fashion. How can anyone measure influence? I can recall kindnesses done to me in my youth by those who have long ago passed to their silent sleep, but who certainly live again. What a desolate world this would be if there was to be life that only existed for its own self.

All that we have, which we call a possession, is in reality but a temporary loan. Ours to love and enjoy for but a brief period. But when anything leaves us to which we have put our touch of love, its enrichment will doubly bless its new and latest guardian.

Photograph © age fotostock/SuperStock

Easter Blooms and Mirthful Tunes

Loise Pinkerton Fritz

I wonder if the flowers grew
upon Mount Calvary,
where Jesus walked
    and bore His cross,
then died for you and me.

Because He was their Maker,
they must have bowed
    their heads
and in their quiet, floral way,
sorrowfully wept.

I wonder if the little birds
all hovered overhead;
they must have sung
    a mournful song
to see the Savior dead.

But, oh, the blooms
    and mirthful tunes
when empty was the grave,
as Jesus Christ, our Savior,
rose upon that Easter Day!

The Easter Story

Alice M. Stewart

Sweetly bloom the Easter lilies,
sending forth a fragrance rare,
telling of a risen Savior,
of His tender love and care.
For as God so clothes the lilies
thus arrayed in purest white,
He is mindful of His children—
He will send what's best
    and right.

Hear the Easter message trilling
from the throats of little birds;
they are telling of God's mercy
in those blithe and tuneful words.

For if He is watching o'er them
and He sees the sparrow fall,
He is caring for His children;
His great love is over all.

Softly blow the Easter breezes
wafting sound of chiming bell;
"O rejoice, for Christ is risen!"
is the story that they tell.
So the birdsong and the lilies,
chime of bells and
    winds that blow,
tell the Resurrection story,
all His lovingkindness show.

The Risen King
Elizabeth Kyle

On the hilltops Easter morning,
sing we praises to the Lord—
He who left the dark tomb empty,
Christ, the glorious living Word.

Hail the blessed risen Savior,
Son of God and Son of man.
Over sin and death triumphant
by His marvelous holy plan.

Let all nations catch the vision
of the Resurrected King.
"Unto Him all praise be given,"
mortal man and angels sing.

Your Easter Song
Minnie Klemme

There's an empty tomb this morning,
for the stone is rolled away.
To Emmaus walks the Savior
on this Happy Easter Day.

Will you meet Him?
    Will you greet Him?
Will you recognize your Lord?
Will you walk in step beside Him?
Will you listen to His Word?

If you do, it will be Easter
all your life and journey long;
"To Emmaus with the Master"—
that will be your Easter song.

Redwood National Park, California.
Photograph © Dennis Frates Photography

The Spire of Hope

Loise Pinkerton Fritz

Across the fields of springtime's wakened green,
a spire of white, stretched heavenward, is seen;

a spire atop God's house, where song and prayer
are lifted up, transcending earthly care;

where, too, from pages of God's Holy Word,
the spoken Easter message still is heard.

Across the fields of springtime's quickened green,
a spire of hope for all mankind is seen.

Christ Is Alive!

Beverly J. Anderson

Rejoice! Rejoice! It's Easter Day;
the angels rolled the stone away.
Christ conquered death and
    sin and strife
to give to us eternal life.

Triumphantly the church bells ring:
"Christ is alive—our risen King!"
Oh, blessed assurance, saving grace,
one day we'll see Him face to face.

Today the message shines anew,
its aged promise ever true.
How can a soul be sad, I say;
for hope was born on Easter Day.

Rejoice! Rejoice! Be glad of heart
for all that Easter doth impart.
Christ is alive! Oh, let us sing
hosannas to our risen King!

Photograph © Charlene Key/Shutterstock

The Joys of Easter

Edith Helstern

Let Easter joys be in your heart;
let skies above be blue;
then may your dearest hopes and dreams
come swiftly, sweetly, true.

And as the Easter days go by,
let all their cheer remain
to echo always in your heart
in loving, glad refrain.

ISBN-13: 978-0-8249-1341-0

Published by Ideals Publications
A Guideposts Company
Nashville, Tennessee
www.idealsbooks.com

Publisher, Peggy Schaefer
Editor, Melinda L. R. Rumbaugh
Copy Editor, Debra Wright
Designer, Marisa Jackson
Permissions Editor, Kristi West

Cover: Stunning tulip display in Keukenhof Garden, Netherlands. Photograph © JacobH/iStockphoto
Inside front cover: *Narcissus* by Starovoitova Nadiia. Image © Starovoitova Nadiia/Shutterstock
Inside back cover: *Tulips* by Kiril Stanchev. Image © Kiril Stanchev/Shutterstock
Additional image credits: "Bits & Pieces," high-angle view of a fence in Lexington, Kentucky. Photograph © Richard Cummins/SuperStock; spot art on back cover, page 1, and "The Story of a Song," and border art for "Family Recipes" by Kathy Rusynyk.
Sheet music for "Christ the Lord Is Risen Today" created by Dick Torrans, Melode, Inc.

Readers are invited to submit original poetry and prose for possible use in future publications. Please send no more than four typed submissions to: Magazine Submissions, Ideals Publications, 2630 Elm Hill Pike, Suite 100, Nashville, Tennessee 37214. Manuscripts will be returned if a self-addressed stamped envelope is included.

ACKNOWLEDGMENTS:

WILSON, RALPH F. "A Broken Cocoon" copyright © Ralph F. Wilson, pastor@joyfulheart.com. All rights reserved. Used by permission. CLARK, WILLIAM. "Easter Parade Limerick"copyright © William Clark www.clarkscript.com. All rights reserved. Used by permission. OUR THANKS to the following authors or their heirs: George Matthew Adams, Beverly J. Anderson, Christa Avampato, Mary A. Barnard, C. Marecy Boring, Gwen Roberts Boyer, Johnielu Barber Bradford, Luella Bender Carr, Ramona K. Cecil, Carol R. Craley, Lois Donovan, Joyce E. Driver , George L. Ehrman, Lois Pinkerton Fritz, Carolyn Winfrey Gillette, Honoria A. Groves, Robert F. Gruenewald, Clay Harrison, Ruth Hazlett, Edith Helstern, Mabel F. Hill, Traci Hutcherson, Pamela Kennedy, Minnie Klemme, Elizabeth Kyle, Helen E. Maynard, Virginia Blanck Moore, Mamie Ozburn Odum, Carol Penner, Florence Weberling Rear, Clara Smith Reber, Alice Kennelly Roberts, Margaret Rorke, Ruth Rouse, Eileen Spinelli, Alice M. Stewart, Susan Sundwall, Wendy Wagner Tousignant, Mary Boyd Wagner, Grace V. Watkins, Kristi J. West, Mabel Marie Wilton.

Scripture quotations, unless otherwise indicated, are taken from King James Version (KJV). Scripture quotations marked NIV1984 are taken from the HOLY BIBLE, NEW INTERNATIONAL VERSION®. Copyright © 1973, 1978, 1984 Biblica. Used by permission of Zondervan. All rights reserved. Scripture marked NKJV taken from the New King James Version®. Copyright © 1982 by Thomas Nelson, Inc. Used by permission. All rights reserved.

Every effort has been made to establish ownership and use of each selection in this book. If contacted, the publisher will be pleased to rectify any inadvertent errors or omissions in subsequent editions.